One day two chicks run away from the hen. They go to the pond and look in the water.

One chick falls in the water. She bobs up and down. She cannot swim. 'Help! Help!'

A duck picks up the chick. He puts her on his back. Then he plays a trick on her.

He swims to a rock in the middle of the pond. He puts the chick on the rock.

The two little chicks jump up and down on the rock in the middle of the pond. 'Cheep, cheep!'

Then he swims back to the grass and picks up the other chick. He puts her on the rock too.

The hen sees them on the rock.

She clucks at the duck to bring them back.

The duck brings the two chicks back to the grass. They are sorry. They will not run away again.